THE BEST OF IT

Also by Kay Ryan

The Jam Jar Lifeboat and
  Other Novelties Exposed

The Niagara River

Say Uncle

Elephant Rocks

Flamingo Watching

Strangely Marked Metal

Dragon Acts to Dragon Ends

THE BEST OF IT

NEW AND SELECTED POEMS

KAY RYAN

GROVE PRESS • NEW YORK

ISBN: 978-0-8021-4521-5

Grove Press
an imprint of Grove/Atlantic, Inc.
841 Broadway
New York, NY 10003

Distributed by Publishers Group West

www.groveatlantic.com

11 12 13   10 9 8 7 6 5 4 3 2

For Carol
who knew it

Contents

ELEPHANT ROCKS
1996

SAY UNCLE
2000

THE NIAGARA RIVER
2005

Acknowledgments

Grateful acknowledgment is made to the following publications in which these previously uncollected poems first appeared:

The American Scholar: Easter Island; Finish

Electronic Poetry Review: Spiderweb

McSweeney's: Dogleg

The New Yorker: The Edges of Time

The Paris Review: Bitter Pill

Parnassus: Virga; Stations; Retroactive

Poetry: Polish and Balm; We're Building the Ship as We Sail It; Train-Track Figure; Pentimenti (*earlier version*); Repetition; Cut Out for It; Bait Goat; Cloud

The Threepenny Review: The Pharaohs; Odd Blocks; Ledge; Still Life with Lemons, Oranges and a Rose

The Yale Review: Galápago

I am grateful to Randy Blasing, editor of Copper Beech Press, who gave my work its first chance and who has now generously allowed many of the poems from *Flamingo Watching* to be reprinted here.

And special thanks to Atsuro Riley who helped me put this manuscript together without Carol.

New Poems

ODD BLOCKS

Every Swiss-village
calendar instructs
as to how stone
gathers the landscape
around it, how
glacier-scattered
thousand-ton
monuments to
randomness become
fixed points in
finding home.
Order is always
starting over.
And why not
also in the self,
the odd blocks,
all lost and left,
become first facts
toward which later
a little town
looks back?

THE EDGES OF TIME

It is at the edges
that time thins.
Time which had been
dense and viscous
as amber suspending
intentions like bees
unseizes them. A
humming begins,
apparently coming
from stacks of
put-off things or
just in back. A
racket of claims now,
as time flattens. A
glittering fan of things
competing to happen,
brilliant and urgent
as fish when seas
retreat.

BAIT GOAT

There is a
distance where
magnets pull,
we feel, having
held them
back. Likewise
there is a
distance where
words attract.
Set one out
like a bait goat
and wait and
seven others
will approach.
But watch out:
roving packs can
pull your word
away. You
find your stake
yanked and some
rough bunch
to thank.

TRAIN-TRACK FIGURE

Imagine a
train-track figure
made of sliver
over sliver of
between-car
vision, each
slice too brief
to add detail
or deepen: that
could be a hat
if it's a person
if it's a person
if it's a person.
Just the same
scant information
timed to supplant
the same scant
information.

WE'RE BUILDING THE SHIP AS WE SAIL IT

The first fear
being drowning, the
ship's first shape
was a raft, which
was hard to unflatten
after that didn't
happen. It's awkward
to have to do one's
planning *in extremis*
in the early years—
so hard to hide later:
sleekening the hull,
making things
more gracious.

VIRGA

There are bands
in the sky where
what happens
matches prayers.
Clouds blacken
and inky rain
hatches the air
like angled writing,
the very transcription
of a pure command,
steady from a steady
hand. Drought
put to rout, visible
a mile above
for miles about.

DOGLEG

Birds' legs
do of course
all dogleg
giving them
that bounce.
But these are
not normal odds
around the house.
Only two of
the dog's legs
dogleg and
two of the cat's.
Fifty-fifty: that's
as bad as it
gets usually,
despite the
fear you feel
when life has
angled brutally.

CLOUD

A blue stain
creeps across
the deep pile
of the evergreens.
From inside the
forest it seems
like an interior
matter, something
wholly to do
with trees, a color
passed from one
to another, a
requirement
to which they
submit unflinchingly
like soldiers or
brave people
getting older.
Then the sun
comes back and
it's totally over.

LEDGE

Birds that love
high trees
and winds
and riding
flailing branches
hate ledges
as gripless
and narrow,
so that a tail
is not just
no advantage
but ridiculous,
mashed vertical
against the wall.
You will have
seen the way
a bird who falls
on skimpy places
lifts into the air
again in seconds—
a gift denied
the rest of us
when our portion
isn't generous.

STATIONS

As the
veldt dries,
the great cats
range farther
to drink,
their paths
looping past
this or that
ex-oasis.
However long
the water's
been gone,
no places
are missed;
despite thirst,
every once-
deep pool
is rehearsed.
It's strange
the way our
route can't be
straightened;

how some
cruel faith
keeps the
stations.

REPETITION

Trying to walk
the same way
to the same
store takes
high-wire balance:
each step not
exactly as
before risks
chasms of
flatness. One
tumble alone
and nothing
happens. Few
are the willing
and fewer
the champions.

THE PHARAOHS

The pharaohs killed those who had built the secret chambers
of the pyramids to ensure that any knowledge of their
existence would be lost.
—Henning Mankell, *The White Lioness*

The moral is
simple: don't
help other people
with their secrets.
But within the
self, what defense
is there against
the pharaohs who
demand chambers
we must build
on pain of death
after which
we're killed?
A person is
as a kingdom
and can afford
some losses toward
the construction of
underground systems,
say the pharaohs,
shutting their
cunning doors
that never were
and won't be
evermore.

PENTIMENTI

"Pentimenti of an earlier position of the arm may be seen."
—Frick Museum

It's not simply
that the top image
wears off or
goes translucent;
things underneath
come back up,
having enjoyed the
advantages of rest.
That's the hardest
part to bear, how
the decided-against
fattens one layer down,
free of the tests
applied to final choices.
In this painting,
for instance, see how
a third arm—
long ago repented
by the artist—
is revealed,

working a flap
into the surface
through which
who knows what
exiled cat or
extra child
might steal.

BITTER PILL

A bitter pill
doesn't need
to be swallowed
to work. Just
reading your name
on the bottle
does the trick.
As though there
were some anti-
placebo effect.
As though the
self were eager
to be wrecked.

POLISH AND BALM

Dust develops
from inside
as well as
on top when
objects stop
being used.
No unguent
can soothe
the chap of
abandonment.
Who knew
the polish
and balm in
a person's
simple passage
among her things.
We knew she
loved them
but not what
love means.

Retroactive

If reward or
amends could
set the clock
back, as happens
in fall when
an hour is stalled
for the sake of light,
then our golgothas
could be put right.
The kiss or reform
or return of the
family farm would
soak into the
injury, ease the
knot of memory,
unname the site
of harm. If there
could be one day
—one hour—of jubilee
how many lame
would walk their property.

Galápago

As one reiterates
oneself day after day,
it's not uncommon
to see nondominant
traits diminish
and the self stray
toward the cartoonish.
As though the self were
a straightening Galápago
where not everything was
going to stay affordable.
Say a stylized struggle
were currently under way
among the finches
whereby the few brighten
while the species vanishes.

FINISH

The grape and plum
might be said to
tarnish when ripe,
developing some
sort of light dust
on their finish
which the least
touch disrupts.
It is this that
the great Dutch
still lifes catch,
the brush as much
in love with talc
as polish. Also
with the strange
seeing-in you notice
when a bruise mars
a fruit's surface.

SHIFT

Words have loyalties
to so much
we don't control.
Each word we write
rights itself
according to poles
we can't see; think of
magnetic compulsion
or an equal stringency.
It's hard for us
to imagine how small
a part we play in
holding up the tall
spires we believe
our minds erect.
Then North shifts,
buildings shear,
and we suspect.

Easter Island

The people of the island built those amazing stone statues, and in the process cut down every last tree. No trees, no wood for houses and fires; no protection from erosion; no useful species, and so on.
—Jon Carroll, *San Francisco Chronicle*

It worked without
a hitch: the last
big head rolled
down the last logs
to its niche.
As planned,
a long chorus
of monoliths
had replaced
the forest, staring
seaward, nicely
spaced, each with
a generous collar
of greensward,
and prepared to
stand so long
that it would be
a good trade: life,
for the thing made.

Cut Out for It

Cut out
as a horse
is cut
from the
pack. Peeled
off, but
a long time
back. Now
such a feeling
for the way
they touch
and shift
as one, the
beauty when
they run.

SPIDERWEB

From other
angles the
fibers look
fragile, but
not from the
spider's, always
hauling coarse
ropes, hitching
lines to the
best posts
possible. It's
heavy work
everyplace,
fighting sag,
winching up
give. It
isn't ever
delicate
to live.

Still Life with Lemons, Oranges and a Rose

(1663) Francisco de Zurbarán

Like two
giant's hands,
shade and
gravity collude
to squeeze away
the light and leave
the clay, rued
Zurbarán. Which
means he has to
find a counter way
to paint, unless he
wants his oranges
too to stick, glued
into a lump
like candy. And
now his wife
is sick.

After Zeno

For my father

When he was
I was.
But I still am
and he is still.

Where is is
when is is was?
I have an is
but where is his?

Now here—
no where:
such a little
fatal pause.

There's no sense
in past tense.

                    1965

FLAMINGO WATCHING

1994

FLAMINGO WATCHING

Wherever the flamingo goes,
she brings a city's worth
of furbelows. She seems
unnatural by nature—
too vivid and peculiar
a structure to be pretty,
and flexible to the point
of oddity. Perched on
those legs, anything she does
seems like an act. Descending
on her egg or draping her head
along her back, she's
too exact and sinuous
to convince an audience
she's serious. The natural elect,
they think, would be less pink,
less able to relax their necks,
less flamboyant in general.
They privately expect that it's some
poorly jointed bland grey animal
with mitts for hands
whom God protects.

THIS LIFE

It's a pickle, this life.
Even shut down to a trickle
it carries every kind of particle
that causes strife on a grander scale:
to be miniature is to be swallowed
by a miniature whale. Zeno knew
the law that we know: no matter
how carefully diminished, a race
can only be *half* finished with success;
then comes the endless halving of the rest—
the ribbon's stalled approach, the helpless
red-faced urgings of the coach.

Extraordinary Lengths

The only justification
for extraordinary lengths
is extraordinary distances.
Yet you don't find this
in the majority of instances.
No, rather you see lengths
swagged from balconies,
ribbons of lengths rippling
languidly, lengths spooling
from enchanted cavities and
grots. Actually there is
hardly a spot of sky or pool
of water uncolored by some
extraordinary length or other.
Brothers fling bolts of gossamer
off buildings with spectacular
results. Birds negotiate an
aerial spaghetti, sure-footed
goats find themselves unsteady.
Poor people in brightly
lacquered boats just help
themselves to lengths
that tangle up and float
as pleasantly as kelp.

Every Painting by Chagall

Every twined groom and bride,
every air fish, smudged Russian,
red horse, yellow chicken, assumes
its position not actually beside
but in some friendly distribution
with a predictable companion.
Every canvas insists on a
similar looseness, each neck
put to at least two uses. And wings
from some bottomless wing source.
They are pleasure wings of course
since any horse or violinist
may mount the blue
simply by wanting to.
(In freedom, dear things
repeat without tedium.)

The Tables Freed

The presence of real objects is a nightmare for me.
I have always overturned objects. A chair or table
turned upside down gives me peace and satisfaction.
—Chagall

A companionable flood can
make things wobble. The
sober table at last enjoys
the bubbles locked in her
grain, straining together
good as Egyptians to shift
the predictable plane.
Dense plates and books
slide off and dive or bloat
but she floats, a legged
boat nosing the helpless
stationaries, the bolted
basin, the metal reliquaries—
in short, the nouns. All over
town tables are bumping
out of doors, negotiating
streets and beginning to
meet at water corners
like packs of mustangs,
blue, red, yellow, stenciled,
enlivened by swells as
wild horses are stretched
liquid and elegant by hills.

LEAVING SPACES

It takes a courageous
person to leave spaces
empty. Certainly any
artist in the Middle Ages
felt this timor, and quickly
covered space over
with griffins, sea serpents,
herbs and brilliant carpets
of flowers—things pleasant
or unpleasant, no matter.
Of course they were cowards
and patronized by cowards
who liked their swards as
filled with birds as leaves.
All of them believed in
sudden edges and completely
barren patches in the mind,
and they didn't want to
think about them all the time.

Periphery

Unlike igneous
crystal-studded
porphyry, famous
since the Egyptian
basin business,
periphery is no
one substance,
but the edges
of anything.
Fountains, for instance,
have a periphery
at some distance
from the spray.
On nice days
idle people circle
all the way around
the central spout.
They do not get wet.
They do not get hot.
If they bring a bottle
they get kicked out, but
generally things are mild
and tolerant at peripheries.
People bring bread the
pigeons eat greedily.

THE MOCK RUIN

. . . built as the backdrop of the stage of the ancient
Roman theatre in Sabratha, Libya, Africa, is the most
perfectly preserved part of the entire structure.
—Ripley's Believe It or Not!

Fakes and mock-ups, stage backdrops
quickly nicked, weathered, and
stuck together for illusion's sake
(getting some parts backwards)
give more, maybe; sway slightly;
take later buffets better generally
than their brittle sources whose
stones were set down in regular courses
and mortared. Maybe there is something
to falseness that doesn't get reported.

Is It Modest?

Is it modest or arrogant
not to enter the scene;
instead to push a parrot
forward or make the air
apparent in the spring;
to press the whole embarrassment
of riches at us, bejeweling
every mean web, glazing
water in ditches; to divest
yourself upon us till
every moth or hibiscus
or bottle fragment is some
aspect of your garment,
some hem to kiss; un-becoming
on and on, leaving us like this?

THE THINGS OF THE WORLD

Wherever the eye lingers
it finds a hunger.
The things of the world
want us for dinner.
Inside each pebble or leaf
or puddle is a hook.
The appetites of the world
compete to catch a look.
What does this mean
and how does it work?
Why aren't rocks complete?
Why isn't green adequate
to green? We aren't gods
whose gaze could save,
but that's how the things
of the world behave.

EMPTINESS

Emptiness cannot be
compressed. Nor can it
fight abuse. Nor is there
an endless West hosting
elk, antelope, and the
tough cayuse. This is
true also of the mind:
it can get used.

SLANT

Can or can't you feel
a dominant handedness
behind the randomness
of loss? Does a skew
insinuate into the
visual plane; do
the avenues begin to
strain for the diagonal?
Maybe there is always
this lean, this slight
slant. Maybe always
a little pressure
on the same rein,
a bias cut to everything,
a certain cant
it's better not to name.

APOLOGY

For E.B.

I thought you were
born to privilege,
some inherited advantage—
like an estate framed
in privet hedge,
or a better-feathered
shuttlecock for badinage,
or other French pretensions.
I never thought you knew about exhaustion—
how we have to leap in the morning
as early as high as possible,
we are so fastened, we are so dutiful.

VACATION

It would be pleasant to walk
in Stonehenge or other places
that have rocks arranged on the
basis of a plan, or plans,
inscrutable to modern man;
to wander among grinders
sunk deep in sheep pastures
or simply set on top Peruvian grit;
to gaze up at incisors
no conceivable jaw could fit;
to stretch to be ignorant enough,
scoured to a clean vessel
as pure as the puzzle, vestal
to a mystery involving people,
but without the heat of people.

A CERTAIN KIND OF EDEN

It seems like you could, but
you can't go back and pull
the roots and runners and replant.
It's all too deep for that.
You've overprized intention,
have mistaken any bent you're given
for control. You thought you chose
the bean and chose the soil.
You even thought you abandoned
one or two gardens. But those things
keep growing where we put them—
if we put them at all.
A certain kind of Eden holds us thrall.
Even the one vine that tendrils out alone
in time turns on its own impulse,
twisting back down its upward course
a strong and then a stronger rope,
the greenest saddest strongest
kind of hope.

No Rest for the Idle

The idle are shackled
to their oars. The waters
of idleness are borderless
of course and must always
be plied. Relief is foreign
on this wide and featureless
ocean. There are no details:
no shores, no tides, no times
when things lift up and then
subside, no sails or smokestacks,
no gravel gathered up and spit back,
no plangencies, no seabirds startled;
the weather, without the Matthew Arnold.

THE NARROW PATH

No rime-grizzled mountain climber,
puzzled by where to put his fingers next,
knows the least thing about
how narrow work gets
that depends only on pleasure.
When it gets late or he gets depressed,
he can hang in a nylon sack,
his whole weight waiting
for the light to come back.
But for people who ascend
only by pleasure
there are no holding straps.
They must keep to the
hairline crack all the time
or fall all the way back.

When Fishing Fails

"Your husband is very lucky," observed Smithers, "to
have ornithology to fall back upon when fishing fails."
—Cyril Hare, *Death Is No Sportsman*

When fishing fails, when no bait avails,
and nothing speaks in liquid hints
of where the fishes went for weeks,
and dimpled ponds and silver creeks
go flat and tarnish, it's nice if
you can finish up your sandwich,
pack your thermos, and ford
this small hiatus toward
a second mild and absorbing purpose.

SAY IT STRAIGHT

I have a mania for straight writing—however
circuitous I may be in what I myself say.
—Marianne Moore

What we would
and what we can say
stray as in a dream;
a certain mad rectitude
creeps in, by which
something simple as an apple
can never be determined
wholly edible.
The crisp act is deferred,
the object blurred by scruples.
The more we cherish clarity
in principle, the more it is
impossible. Will enamel
ever strike the fruit?
Will Eve grow wild and forgivable?
For it's unlovable
to talk too long with snakes,
whose reasons fork
the more the more
she hesitates.

GLASS SLIPPERS

Despite the hard luck
of the ugly stepsisters,
most people's feet will fit
into glass slippers.
The arch rises, the heel
tapers, the toes align
in descending order
and the whole thing slides
without talcum powder
into the test slipper.
We *can* shape to the
dreams of another; we are
eager to yield. It is a
mutual pleasure to the holder
of the slipper and to the
foot held. It is a singular
moment—tender, improbable,
and as yet unclouded by the
problems that hobble the pair
when they discover that
the matching slipper

isn't anywhere, nor does
the bare foot even share
the shape of the other.
When they compare,
the slippered foot makes
the other odder: it looks
like a hoof. So many miracles
don't start far back enough.

How Successful Can She Afford to Be?

Maybe the mime's test
would be to get you to drink
from the glass she passed.

What if you did
grasp it just right;
what if it did flash
in the window light?

Would she be glad
if it left a ring,
if she could
add to the manifest,
passing a thing
out of the dream?

How close to the door
can she lean,
how genuinely bid you enter,
where she herself is a guest
on her best behavior?

REPETITION

First the mind does something
to see if it can.
Then the mind does the same thing
because it can.
But there is mind left over:
the excited part.
This is the poison in repetition.
But it is a very weak poison
and no reason to forego
the deep abiding consolations
of repetition. The poison
may build up usefully,
as it built up in the Egyptians—
a preservative. What will ever
equal accretion's extravagance?
Take the grand conservative temples
to the golden Horus-headed pharaohs,
for instance.

LES NATURES
PROFONDEMENT BONNES SONT
TOUJOURS INDÉCISES

One strong squirt
of will and the world
fills with direction.
All roads go Roman.
The path not taken
is not kept open.
There is suddenly
a rational waterworks
system. Things are done
as no indecisive person
could do them. Still
there is a population
that likes mistakes and
indecision, guarding
atavisms and anatomical
sports, the hips of snakes,
the wings of the horse.
They do not argue that
this is useful. They
make no mention of the
gene pool. They just
like to think about
these things. They
make them comfortable.

So Different

A tree is lightly connected
to its blossoms.
For a tree it is
a pleasant sensation
to be stripped
of what's white and winsome.
If a big wind comes,
any nascent interest in fruit
scatters. This is so different
from humans, for whom
what is un-set matters
so oddly—as though
only what is lost held possibility.

HALF A LOAF

The whole loaf's loft
is halved in profile,
like the standing side
of a bombed cathedral.

The cut face
of half a loaf
puckers a little.

The bread cells
are open and brittle
like touching coral.

It is nothing like the middle
of an uncut loaf,
nothing like a conceptual half
which stays moist.

I say do not adjust to half
unless you must.

Soft

In harmony with the rule of irony—
which requires that we harbor the enemy
on this side of the barricade—the shell
of the unborn eagle or pelican, which is made
to give protection till the great beaks can harden,
is the first thing to take up poison.
The mineral case is soft and gibbous
as the moon in a lake—an elastic,
rubbery, nightmare water that won't break.
Elsewhere, also, I see the mockeries of struggle,
a softness over people.

SPRING

Winter, like a set opinion,
is routed. What gets it out?
The imposition of some external season
or some internal doubt?
I see the yellow maculations spread
across bleak hills of what I said
I'd always think; a stippling of white
upon the grey; a pink the shade
of what I said I'd never say.

I Marveled at How Generally I Was Aided

—The Autobiography of Charles Darwin

I marvel at how generally
I am aided, how frequently
the availability of help
is demonstrated. I've had
unbridgeable distances collapse
and opposite objects coalesce
enough to think duress itself
may be a prayer. Perhaps not chance,
but need, selects; and desperation
works upon giraffes until their necks
can reach the necessary branch.
If so, help alters; makes seven vertebrae
go farther in the living generation;
help coming to us, not from the fathers,
not to the children.

IMPERSONAL

The working kabbalist
resists the lure of
the personal. She
suspends interest
in the biblical list
of interdicted shellfish,
say, in order to
read the text another way.
It might seem to some
superficial to convert
letters to numerals
or in general refuse plot
in favor of dots or half circles;
it might easily seem
comical, how she
ignores an obviously
erotic tale except for
every third word,
rising for her like braille
for something vivid
as only the impersonal

can be—a crescent
bright as the moon,
a glimpse of a symmetry,
a message so vast
in its passage that
she must be utterly open
to an alien idea of person.

A Certain Meanness
of Culture

*And about Blake's supernatural territories, as about the
supposed ideas that dwell there, we cannot help commenting
on a certain meanness of culture. They illustrate the cranki-
ness, the eccentricity, which frequently affects writers outside
of the Latin tradition.*
—T. S. Eliot

What else can we do,
born on deserts
occupied haphazard
by borax traders
aspiring to a
stucco elegance
if they're real lucky?
Someone has to get here
before the mythology,
to be happy in the
first tailings of industry,
and of course lonely
and susceptible to
the opinions of donkeys
since donkeys are the
main company out here
among the claims.
Snakes and wild things
skitter off too fast
for conversation.
You can get an appreciation
for why a donkey is
fussy about books
since she carries them.

You start to value culture
like you would water.
I'd say this one's about
a two-cupper. And when
you dream, it's not romance.
Things are too thin
out here already to chance
sad endings. You get
pretty stringy and impatient
with the fat smoke off
old cities. You get cranky
and admire just what stands up
to the stars' cold and the
sun's fire. You like winches
and pulleys, picks and khakis,
and the rare sweet grass you can
find for your donkey.

THE TEST WE SET OURSELF

An honest work generates its own power; a dishonest work
tries to rob power from the cataracts of the given.
—Annie Dillard

If we could be less human,
if we could stand out of the range
of the cataracts of the given,
and not find our pockets swollen
with change we haven't—but must have—
stolen, who wouldn't?
It isn't a gift; we are beholden
to the sources we crib—
always something's overflow,
or someone's rib hidden in our breast;
the answer sewn inside us
that invalidates the test we set ourself
against the boneless angel at our right
and at our left the elf.

FORCE

Nothing forced works.
The Gordian knot just worsens
if it's jerked at by a person.
One of the main stations
of the cross is patience.
Another, of course, is impatience.
There is such a thing as
too much tolerance
for unpleasant situations,
a time when the gentle
teasing out of threads
ceases to be pleasing
to a woman born for conquest.
Instead she must assault
the knot or alp or everest
with something sharp
and take upon herself
the moral warp of sudden progress.

MINERS' CANARIES

It isn't arbitrary;
it isn't curious;
miners' canaries
serve ordinary purposes
with just a fillip of
extra irony.
Something is always
testing the edges
of the breathable—
not so sweet, not so yellow,
but something is always
living at the wrong edge
of the arable; something
is always excused first
from the water table,
chalking the boundary
of the possible
from the far side;
even in the individual.

THE HINGE OF SPRING

The jackrabbit is a mild herbivore
grazing the desert floor,
quietly abridging spring,
eating the color off everything
rampant-height or lower.

Rabbits are one of the things
coyotes are for. One quick scream,
a few quick thumps,
and a whole little area
shoots up blue and orange clumps.

Deer

To lure a single swivel ear,
one tentative twig of a leg,
or a nervous tail here,
is to mark this place
as the emperor's park,
rife, I say rife, with deer.
For if one leaf against the littered floor
be cleft with the true arc,
all this lost ground, and more,
becomes a park. Everywhere
the nearest deer signals the nearest dark.
A buck looks up: the touch of his rack
against wet bark whispers a syllable
singular to deer; the next one hears
and shifts; the next head stops
and lifts; deeper and deeper into the park.

Sheep in Wolves' Clothing

Of all the unpleasant
affectations of soi-disant
wolves, the most unpleasant
is their teeth: blunt ruminant
sheep stumps built up
to something no one could
really kill with. Decorative
in the worst sense. An offense
to economy and outright
blasphemy in the context
of true wolf philosophy,
which states very clearly
that every bluff must
promote good. Which means
you eat what you've fooled:
all of Little Red Riding,
from her shoes to her hood.

Snake Charm

Oh for even a fingerling snake,
a three-inch inspiration full of
genetic information about length,
the making of venom, and the start
of muscles later on used for compression.
A snake, say, in a Moorish pattern, abstract,
ornamental, repeatable over a whole Toledo
without tedium. Yes, a snake the sun stretches,
a snake that improves everything it catches:
the adventitious mouse converted to stripes
or diamond patches. This snake is reckless,
with no concern for balance. It can
slide over any surface, a silent line,
an endless pattern, a generative rhyme.

THE PALM AT THE END
OF THE MIND

After fulfilling everything
one two three he came back again
free, no more prophecy requiring
that he enter the city just this way,
no more set-up treacheries.
It was the day after Easter. He adored
the eggshell litter and the cellophane
caught in the grass. Each door he passed
swung with its own business, all the
witnesses along his route of pain
again distracted by fear of loss
or hope of gain. It was wonderful
to be a man, bewildered by
so many flowers, the rush
and ebb of hours, his own
ambiguous gestures—his
whole heart exposed, then
taking cover.

POETRY IS A KIND OF MONEY

Poetry is a kind of money
whose value depends upon reserves.
It's not the paper it's written on
or its self-announced denomination,
but the bullion, sweated from the earth
and hidden, which preserves its worth.
Nobody knows how this works,
and how can it? Why does something
stacked in some secret bank or cabinet,
some miser's trove, far back, lambent,
and gloated over by its golem, make us
so solemnly convinced of the transaction
when Mandelstam says *gold,* even
in translation?

PERSIFLAGE

Garden serpents
small as shoelaces
are found in
side lots and
grassy places.
Green coat
striped with yellow
makes the garden viper
a dapper fellow.
Birds mock
and children chase
our minor adder
thinner than a pencil.
Born sans puff or rattle
he counts on persiflage
in battle. Before
his flippant tongue
children stiffen,
dogs fall like
beef cattle.

MASTERWORKS OF MING

Ming, Ming,
such a lovely
thing blue
and white

bowls and
basins glow
in museum
light

they would
be lovely
filled with
rice or
water

so nice
adjunct
to dinner

or washing
a daughter

a small
daughter
of course
since it's
a small basin

first you
would put
one then

the other
end in.

BREAST BIRDS

Breast birds don't breed true.
Once you let them out of you
their vividness is brief;
their orange or blue
fades back to brown
as quick as your relief.
Oh love, oh loneliness, oh grief.

Paired Things

Who, who had only seen wings,
could extrapolate the
skinny sticks of things
birds use for land,
the backward way they bend,
the silly way they stand?
And who, only studying
bird tracks in the sand,
could think those little forks
had decamped on the wind?
So many paired things seem odd.
Who ever would have dreamed
the broad winged raven of despair
would quit the air and go
bandy-legged upon the ground,
a common crow?

OSPREY

The great taloned osprey
nests in Scotland.
Her nest's the biggest
thing around, a spiked basket
with hungry ugly osprey offspring
in it. For months she sits on it.
He fishes, riding four-pound salmon
home like rockets. They get
all the way there before they die,
so muscular and brilliant
swimming through the sky.

TURTLE

Who would be a turtle who could help it?
A barely mobile hard roll, a four-oared helmet,
she can ill afford the chances she must take
in rowing toward the grasses that she eats.
Her track is graceless, like dragging
a packing case places, and almost any slope
defeats her modest hopes. Even being practical,
she's often stuck up to the axle on her way
to something edible. With everything optimal,
she skirts the ditch which would convert
her shell into a serving dish. She lives
below luck-level, never imagining some lottery
will change her load of pottery to wings.
Her only levity is patience,
the sport of truly chastened things.

ELEPHANT ROCKS
1996

Living with Stripes

In tigers, zebras,
and other striped creatures,
any casual posture
plays one beautiful set of lines
against another:
herringbones and arrows
appear and disappear;
chevrons widen and narrow.
Miniature themes and counterpoints
occur in the flexing and extending
of the smaller joints.
How can they stand to drink,
when lapping further complicates
the way the water duplicates their lines?
Knowing how their heads will zigzag out,
I wonder if they dread to start sometimes.

DOUBT

A chick has just so much time
to chip its way out, just so much
egg energy to apply to the weakest spot
or whatever spot it started at.
It can't afford doubt. Who can?
Doubt uses albumen
at twice the rate of work.
One backward look by any of us
can cost what it cost Orpheus.
Neither may you answer
the stranger's knock;
you know it is the Person from Porlock
who eats dreams for dinner,
his napkin stained the most delicate colors.

Mirage Oases

First among places
susceptible to trespass
are mirage oases

whose graduated pools
and shaded grasses, palms,
and speckled fishes give
before the lightest pressure
and are wrecked.

For they live
only in the kingdom
of suspended wishes,

thrive only at our pleasure
checked.

Cirque

Even the clean
blue-green water
of the cirque,
with nothing
in between
the snow and it
but slant,
can't speed
the work,
must wait
upon whatever
makes it white
to dissipate.
It seems
so hard to think
that even lakes
so pure
should start opaque,
that something
always
has to recombine
or sink.

Chemistry

Words especially
are subject to
the chemistry
of death: it is
an acid bath
which dissolves
or doubles
their strength.
Sentiments
which pleased
drift down
as sediment;
iron trees
grow from filament.

THAT VASE OF LILACS

Not just lilacs
are like that;
other purples also
leave us vacant
portals, susceptible
to vagrant spirits.
But take that vase
of lilacs: who goes
near it is erased.
In spite of Proust,
the senses don't
attach us to a place
or time: we're *used*
by sweetness—
taken, defenseless,
invaded by a line
of Saracens,
Picts, Angles,

double rows of
fragrance-loving
ancients—people
matched casually
by nose in an
impersonal and
intermittent immortality
of purple.

CONNECTIONS

Connections *lie in wait*—
something that in
the ordinary line of offenses
makes offense more great.
They entrap, they solicit
under false pretenses,
they premeditate.
They tie one of
your shoelaces
to one of a stranger,
they tie strings to purses
and snatch as
you lean down, eager
for a little something gratis.

DEW

As neatly as peas
in their green canoe,
as discretely as beads
strung in a row,
sit drops of dew
along a blade of grass.
But unattached and
subject to their weight,
they slip if they accumulate.
Down the green tongue
out of the morning sun
into the general damp,
they're gone.

LACQUER ARTIST

There is a nacreous gleam
in certain areas of the mind
where something must have been
at some time—
perhaps many somethings,
judging by the pearlescence;
maybe the same weightless pleasures
or the same elusive lessons
repeated and repeated
with the patience
of the lacquer artist seated
at his task—eighty
coats per Japanese box.

All Shall Be Restored

The grains shall be collected
from the thousand shores
to which they found their way,
and the boulder restored,
and the boulder itself replaced
in the cliff, and likewise
the cliff shall rise
or subside until the plate of earth
is without fissure. Restoration
knows no half-measure. It will
not stop when the treasured and lost
bronze horse remounts the steps.
Even this horse will founder backward
to coin, cannon, and domestic pots,
which themselves shall bubble and
drain back to green veins in stone.
And every word written shall lift off
letter by letter, the backward text
read ever briefer, ever more antic
in its effort to insist that nothing
shall be lost.

FULL MEASURE

You will get your full measure.
But, as when asking fairies for favors,
there is a trick: it comes in a block.
And of course one block is not
like another. Some respond to water,
giving everything wet a little flavor.
Some succumb to heat, like butter.
Others give to steady pressure.
Others shatter at a tap. But
some resist; nothing in nature softens up
their bulk and no personal attack works.
People whose gift will not break
live by it all their lives; it shadows
every empty act they undertake.

STARS OF BETHLEHEMS

Throughout the sky
there are cinders
black as the night.
These are unborn stars
awaiting their source of light.

The night is gritty
with things to hit,
should something
go on in a city
or the outskirts of it.

CRIB

From the Greek for
woven or *plaited,*
which quickly translated
to *basket.* Whence the verb
crib, which meant "to filch"
under cover of wicker
anything—some liquor,
a cutlet.
For we want to make off
with things that are not
our own. There is a pleasure
theft brings, a vitality
to the home.
Cribbed objects or answers
keep their guilty shimmer
forever, have you noticed?
Yet religions downplay this.
Note, for instance, in our
annual rehearsals of innocence,
the substitution of *manger* for *crib*—
as if we ever deserved that baby,
or thought we did.

BESTIARY

A bestiary catalogs
bests. The mediocres
both higher and lower
are suppressed in favor
of the singularly savage
or clever, the spectacularly
pincered, the archest
of the arch deceivers
who press their advantage
without quarter even after
they've won, as of course they would.
Best is not to be confused with *good*—
a different creature altogether,
and treated of in the goodiary—
a text alas lost now for centuries.

How Birds Sing

One is not taxed;
one need not practice;
one simply tips
the throat back
over the spine axis
and asserts the chest.
The wings and the rest
compress a musical
squeeze which floats
a series of notes
upon the breeze.

How a Thought Thinks

A thought is dumb,
without eyes, ears,
opposable thumb,
or a tongue.
A thought lives
underground, not
wholly mole-ish
but with some
of the same
disinterests.
The amazing thing
is that it isn't helpless.
Of all creatures
it is the most
random eater.
Caring only for travel
it eats whatever
roots, ants, or gravel
it meets. It occupies
no more space
than moles. We know it
only by some holes
and the way
apparently healthy notions
topple in the garden.

INTENTION

Intention doesn't sweeten.
It should be picked young
and eaten. Sometimes only hours
separate the cotyledon
from the wooden plant.
Then if you want to eat it,
you can't.

If the Moon Happened Once

If the moon happened *once*,
it wouldn't matter much,
would it?

One evening's ticket
punched with a
round or a crescent.

You could like it
or not like it,
as you chose.

It couldn't alter
every time it rose;

it couldn't do those
things with scarves
it does.

NEW CLOTHES

The emperor who
was tricked by the tailors
is familiar to you.

But the tailors
keep on changing
what they do
to make money.

(*Tailor* means
to make something
fit somebody.)

Be guaranteed
that they will discover
your pride.

You will cast aside
something you cherish
when the tailors whisper,
"*Only you could wear this.*"

It is almost never clothes
such as the emperor bought

but it is always something close
to something you've got.

SIMPLY BY GROWING LARGER

*Simply by growing larger, any object will suffer continual
decrease in relative surface area.*
—Stephen Jay Gould

As a thing grows larger,
it grows darker.
The dense organs flourish.
More and more blood goes to nourish
the purplish lobes
and loops of sausage,
all slickly packaged.
Once-agile limbs are now fragile
Humpty-Dumpty legs and arms.
Whatever charms the small thing had
are history. This is
particularly cruel in spring,
when simpler hearts can
flush and blanch a pair of wings
in one exchange, and sense
is one cell deep, and things
aren't sullied. Then it is strange
to be the one who chanced to keep,
to grow gravid and broad-bellied.

To the Young Anglerfish

The angler's lure required five hundred separate modifications to attain its exquisite mimicry.
—Stephen Jay Gould

For now and for the next 400-plus generations,
the hornlike symptom on your brow
will itch and be subject to irritation.
At that point it will begin to resemble a modification
useful for tricking food. It will at last begin
to begin to do some good.
Meanwhile, the problems of life enhance:
an awkwardness attends the mating dance
and an inexplicable thoughtfulness
at the wrong moments.
That part of you that is pledged to the future
abstracts you in some way from nature
with the small *n*. You feel a
comical budding power, and then
you don't again.

CRUSTACEAN ISLAND

There could be an island paradise
where crustaceans prevail.
Click, click, go the lobsters
with their china mitts and
articulated tails.
It would not be sad like whales
with their immense and patient sieving
and the sobering modesty
of their general way of living.
It would be an island blessed
with only cold-blooded residents
and no human angle.
It would echo with a thousand castanets
and no flamencos.

Imaginary Eskimos

Who knows
if Eskimos
choose to go
with floes
or just go,
regretting motion,
missing a fixed position
vis-à-vis the ocean.
It is common
to suppose
that anyone
whom one is not
is predisposed
to like her lot—
that when she
drills down
through the ice
to fish
and sees the black
and restless drift
and works against
the cold occlusion
which always threatens,
it is easier
for that sort of person.

OUTSIDER ART

Most of it's too dreary
or too cherry red.
If it's a chair, it's
covered with things
the Savior said
or should have said—
dense admonishments
in nail polish
too small to be read.
If it's a picture,
the frame is either
burnt matches glued together
or a regular frame painted over
to extend the picture. There never
seems to be a surface equal
to the needs of these people.
Their purpose wraps
around the backs of things
and under arms;
they gouge and hatch

and glue on charms
till likable materials—
apple crates and canning funnels—
lose their rural ease. We are not
pleased the way we thought
we would be pleased.

LES PETITES CONFITURES

(*The Little Jams*)

These three pieces
in Satie's elegant notation
were just discovered
at the Métro station
where he rolled them
in a *Figaro* of April twenty-second,
nineteen twenty-seven,
and put them in a pipe
two inches in diameter, the type
then commonly used for banisters.
They are three sticky pieces
for piano or banjo—
each instrument to be played
so as to sound like the other.
That is really the hub
of the amusement. Each piece
lasts about a minute.
When they were first tried
after being in the pipe,
they kept rolling back up.
Really, keeping them flat
was half the banjo-piano
man's work.

WHY ISN'T IT ALL MORE MARKED

Why isn't it all
more marked,
why isn't every wall
graffitied, every park tree
stripped like the
stark limbs
in the house of
the chimpanzees?
Why is there bark
left? Why do people
cling to their
shortening shrifts
like rafts? So
silent.
Not why people *are;*
why not *more* violent?
We must be
so absorbent.
We must be
almost crystals,

almost all some
neutralizing chemical
that really does
clarify and bring peace,
take black sorrow
and make surcease.

WITNESS

Never trust a witness.
By the time a thing is
noticed, it has happened.
Some magician's redirected
our attention to the rabbit.
The best life is suspected,
not examined.
And never trust reverse.
The mourners of the dead
count backward from the date
of the event, rehearsing
its approach, investing
final words with greatest weight,
as though weight ever
carried what we meant;
as though he could have
told us where he went.

LEARNING

Whatever must be learned
is always on the bottom,
as with the law of drawers
and the necessary item.
It isn't pleasant,
whatever they tell children,
to turn out on the floor
the folded things in them.

Apogee

At high speeds
we know
when an orbit
starts to go
backwards:
on fair rides
like the Hammer
or in airplane disasters,
our brains are
plastered to
one wall of the skull
or another;
we comprehend reverse
through the
sudden compression
of matter.
In a way it's worse
when the turn's wider—
say a boat on a soft tide
in mild water—
we hardly knew
that we were floating out.
The sense of turning back
seems like our fault.

AGAINST GRAVITY

How do we move
under weight?
What opposite force
do we generate
that keeps our clothes
floating around us,
for instance, or goes
any distance toward
explaining our fondness
for jumping?
Some pump,
like a fish tank's, maybe;
some auto-aeration or something.
Because we're glad some mornings,
and buoyant, as though we had
no bombs or appointments.

LACUNAE

Lacunae aren't
what was going to be
empty anyway.
They aren't spaces
with uses, such as
margins or highway edges.
Lacunae are losses
in the middles of places—
drops where something
documented happened
but the document is
gone—pond shaped
or jagged.

INTRANSIGENCE

Intransigence is the main fault—or the great virtue—
of the Saties.
—Pierre-Daniel Templier, *Erik Satie*

Intransigence
as a quality
rejects influence
and encourages oddity.

I will not be moved
it says most movingly
to anyone
touched by irony.

For intransigence
lives in a host
and like all guests
must pay a cost.

It is worn
and worked at by mortality.
The flesh erodes
beneath it gradually.

What was fierce
becomes cantankerous.
It is cruel for the host
and for intransigence.

AGE

As some people age
they kinden.
The apertures
of their eyes widen.
I do not think they weaken;
I think something weak strengthens
until they are more and more it,
like letting in heaven.
But other people are
mussels or clams, frightened.
Steam or knife blades mean open.
They hear heaven, they think boiled or broken.

COUNSEL

It is possible
that even the best counsel
cannot be processed
by the body.
All supplements to
our personal chemistry
are screened by tiny
fanatical secret organs
that refuse much more than
they accept. It is hard
to add even minerals.
Iron tablets, for example,
are not correct
and pass through us like
windowless alien crafts.
What the body wants is so exact.

INSULT

Insult is injury
taken personally,
saying, *This is not*
a random fracture
that would have happened
to any leg out there;
this was a conscious unkindness.
We need insult to remind us
that we aren't always just hurt,
that there are some sources—
even in the self—parts of which
tread on other parts with such boldness
that we must say, *You must stop this.*

SILENCE

Silence is not snow.
It cannot grow
deeper. A thousand years
of it are thinner
than paper. So
we must have it
all wrong
when we feel trapped
like mastodons.

A Cat/A Future

A cat can draw
the blinds
behind her eyes
whenever she
decides. Nothing
alters in the stare
itself but she's
not there. Likewise
a future can occlude:
still sitting there,
doing nothing rude.

HOPE

What's the use
of something
as unstable
and diffuse as hope—
the almost-twin
of making do,
the isotope
of going on:
what isn't in
the envelope
just before
it isn't:
the always tabled
righting of the present.

LOSSES

Most losses add something—
a new socket or silence,
a gap in a personal
archipelago of islands.

We have that difference
to visit—itself
a going-on of sorts.

But there are other losses
so far beyond report
that they leave holes
in holes only

like the ends of the
long and lonely lives
of castaways
thought dead but not.

The Cabinet of Curiosities

It's hard for
minor monsters
born with more
of one thing
than others—
the curse of
double vision
in a single head,
or double ears.
If they are people
their careers
are always troubled—
self-accused,
God-hobbled—
the spilling cup
they took for a blessing—
their lives spent
mopping up,
apologizing.

HER POLITENESS

It's her politeness
one loathes: how she
isn't insistent, how
she won't impose, how
nothing's so urgent
it won't wait. Like
a meek guest you tolerate
she goes her way—the muse
you'd have leap at your throat,
you'd spring to obey.

BAD PATCH

It is not comical like grease
with its brief release from traction
where a Model T spins off
and liberates a crate of chickens
to the cooking pots of poor Italians.
It was not witnessed.
There was no vehicle.
It is too late
to call for sets,
hire on people.

SWEPT UP WHOLE

You aren't *swept up whole,*
however it feels. You're
atomized. The wind passes.
You recongeal. It's
a surprise.

ANY MORNING

Any morning
can turn molten
without warning.
Every object
can grow fluent.
Suddenly the kitchen
has a sulfur river
through it;
there is a burping
from the closet,
a release of
caustic gases
from the
orange juice glasses.
The large appliances
are bonding in a way
that isn't pleasant
on linoleum as friable
as bacon. We never
fathom how we caused it,
or why we
never see it coming
like Hawaii.

RELIEF

We know it is close
to something lofty.
Simply getting over being sick
or finding lost property
has in it the leap,
the purge, the quick humility
of witnessing a birth—
how love seeps up
and retakes the earth.
There is a dreamy
wading feeling to your walk
inside the current
of restored riches,
clocks set back,
disasters averted.

Part Midas

The trick would be to be
part Midas—to have
a switch inside us
we could flick at our
pleasure. It would be
nice to plate a chalice
or turn the neighbor's dog
to treasure or add
mettle to lettuce—
to practice playful
acts of malice, table-
top amusements—
stopping short
of where the goblets
started breeding goblets.

The Woman Who Wrote Too Much

I have written
over the doors
of the various
houses and stores
where friends
and supplies were.

Now I can't
locate them anymore
and must shout
general appeals
in the street.

It is a miracle
to me now—
when a piece
of the structure unseals

and there is a dear one,
coming out,
with something
for me to eat.

SONNET TO SPRING

The brown, unpleasant,
aggressively ribbed and
unpliant leaves of the loquat,
shaped like bark canoes that
something squashed flat,
litter the spring cement.
A fat-cheeked whim of air—
a French *vent* or some similar affair—
with enough choices in the front yard
for a blossomy puff worthy of Fragonard,
instead expends its single breath
beneath one leathery leaf of loquat
which flops over and again lies flat.
Spring is frivolous like that.

A Plain Ordinary Steel Needle
Can Float on Pure Water

—Ripley's Believe It or Not

Who hasn't seen
a plain ordinary
steel needle float serene
on water as if lying on a pillow?
The water cuddles up like Jell-O.
It's a treat to see water
so rubbery, a needle
so peaceful, the point encased
in the tenderest dimple.
It seems so *simple*
when things or people
have modified each other's qualities
somewhat;
we almost forget the oddity
of that.

DISTANCE

The texts
are insistent:
it takes two points
to make a distance.

The cubit,
for instance,
is nothing
till you use it.

Then it is rigid
and bracelike;
it has actual strength.

Something metal
runs through
every length—

the very armature
of love, perhaps.

Only distance
lets distance collapse.

The Vessel and the Cup

From a Hasidic story

What cup knows the distress
of the large vessel, knows
any more than two inches
of the purple? For the cup,
everything that fills it up
is equal—the little jug,
the pot, the large vessel.
Beyond its own meniscus
nothing's knowable for a cup.
But the vessel wishes
one something
could use it up.

WOODEN

In the presence of supple
goodness, some people
grow less flexible,
experiencing a woodenness
they wouldn't have thought possible.
It is as strange and paradoxical
as the combined suffering
of Pinocchio and Geppetto
if Pinocchio had turned and said,
I can't be human after all.

The Second

In any collision, one strikes;
the other is stricken. This
is a given with the nano-
calculations made possible
through silicon.
Earlier centuries depended
on testimony to know
the bender from the bent
and often judged an act
by how it ended. Many bumps
were simply abandoned to the
morass of simultaneous action.
Love being among them.
For who would be second
as I find myself second—
the original feathered weapon
tattered, *I love you* seconded
for seven years. Whose love
comes second forever bears
a quiver of unsayable words,
unusable gestures; a boldness
lost—as if Ruth had not said,
Whither thou goest, but merely gone,
making Naomi's people her people,
her home her home.

HEAT

There is a heat
coming off
anything we meet
our-sized and
mildly round.
Who has not found
herself warmed
by certain stones,
for example, or
made occasional
"mistakes" about things
that didn't turn out
to be people?
Perhaps we
share a shape
that loves itself,
a heat anterior
to life, further back
than hearts.
I postulate
a very early date
for when the warming
starts.

POETRY IN TRANSLATION

It is
so snug—
the skin
of the living animal
stretched out
to a rug
shaped something
like the United States.
One meditates
upon a
Florida-like flap—
a forward leg
which ran
the Russian steppes
perhaps?

IF SHE ONLY HAD ONE MINUTE

What would she put in it?
She wouldn't *put*
she thinks; she would *take,*
suck it up
like a deep lake—
bloat indiscriminate
on her last instant—
feast on everything she
had released, dismissed, or
pushed away; she would make
room and room as though
her whole life of resistance
had been for this one purpose:
on the last minute of the last day
she would drink and have it; ballooning
like a gravid salmon or the moon.

Elephant Rocks

Here and there,
at the edges and marges,
a bit of an elephant surfaces—
a dome and a dip, a haunch
or an aspect of head—
some worn-away soft and yet
angular hump of the
shambling elephant armature,
up through the earth—a bump
or a knob with the elephant signature.
The ancient, implacable creature
comes ambling back; a bulge
reemerges, that sober, that
giveaway grey. The dirt
rubs away from a treasure
too patient and deep to be lost,
however we've hurt, whatever
we've done to the beasts,
whatever we say.

SAY UNCLE

2000

SAY UNCLE

Every day
you say,
*Just one
more try.*
Then another
irrecoverable
day slips by.
You will
say *ankle,*
you will
say *knuckle;*
why won't
you why
won't you
say *uncle?*

CORNERS

All but saints
and hermits
mean to paint
themselves
toward an exit

leaving a
pleasant ocean
of azure or jonquil
ending neatly
at the doorsill.

But sometimes
something happens:

a minor dislocation
by which the doors
and windows
undergo a
small rotation
to the left a little

—but repeatedly.
It isn't
obvious immediately.

Only toward evening
and from the
farthest corners
of the houses
of the painters

comes a chorus
of individual keening
as of kenneled dogs
someone is mistreating.

STAR BLOCK

There is no such thing
as *star block*.
We do not think of
locking out the light
of other galaxies.
It is light
so rinsed of impurities
(heat, for instance)
that it excites
no antibodies in us.
Yet people are
curiously soluble
in starlight.
Bathed in its
absence of insistence
their substance
loosens willingly,
their bright
designs dissolve.
Not proximity
but distance
burns us with love.

MOCKINGBIRD

Nothing whole
is so bold,
we sense. Nothing
not cracked is
so exact and
of a piece. He's
the distempered
emperor of parts,
the king of patch,
the master of
pastiche, who so
hashes other birds'
laments, so minces
their capriccios, that
the dazzle of dispatch
displaces the originals.
As though brio
really does beat feeling,
the way two aces
beat three hearts
when it's cards
you're dealing.

A Hundred Bolts of Satin

All you
have to lose
is one
connection
and the mind
uncouples
all the way back.
It seems
to have been
a train.
There seems
to have been
a track.
The things
that you
unpack
from the
abandoned cars
cannot sustain
life: a crate of
tractor axles,
for example,

a dozen dozen
clasp knives,
a hundred
bolts of satin—
perhaps you
specialized
more than
you imagined.

The Excluded Animals

Only a certain
claque of beasts
is part of the
crèche racket

forming a
steamy-breathed
semicircle
around the
baby basket.

Anything more
exotic than
a camel
is out of luck
this season.

Not that the
excluded animals envy
the long-lashed
sycophants;

cormorants
don't toady,
nor do toads
adore anybody
for any reason.

Nor do the
unchosen alligators,
grinning their
three-foot grin
as they laze
in the blankety waters
like the blankets on Him.

BLANDEUR

If it please God,
let less happen.
Even out Earth's
rondure, flatten
Eiger, blanden
the Grand Canyon.
Make valleys
slightly higher,
widen fissures
to arable land,
remand your
terrible glaciers
and silence
their calving,
halving or doubling
all geographical features
toward the mean.
Unlean against our hearts.
Withdraw your grandeur
from these parts.

Composition

Language is a diluted aspect of matter.
—Joseph Brodsky

No. Not *diluted.*
Flaked; wafered;
but not watered.
Language is matter
leafing like a book
with the good taste
of rust and exposure
the way ironwork
petals near the coast.
But so many more
colors than rust:
or, argent, others—
a vast heraldic shield
of beautiful readable
fragments revealed
as Earth delaminates:
how the metals scatter,
how matter turns
animate.

PATIENCE

Patience is
wider than one
once envisioned,
with ribbons
of rivers
and distant
ranges and
tasks undertaken
and finished
with modest
relish by
natives in their
native dress.
Who would
have guessed
it possible
that waiting
is sustainable—
a place with
its own harvests.
Or that in
time's fullness

the diamonds
of patience
couldn't be
distinguished
from the genuine
in brilliance
or hardness.

Coming and Going

There is a
recently discovered
order, neither
sponges nor fishes,
which is never
at the mercy
of conditions.
If currents shift,
these fleshy zeppelins
can reverse directions
from inside—
their guts are
so easily modified.
Coming versus going
is therefore
not the crisis
it is for people,
who have to scramble
to keep anything
from showing
when we see
what we can't see
coming, going.

NOTHING VENTURED

Nothing exists as a block
and cannot be parceled up.
So if nothing's ventured
it's not just talk;
it's the big wager.
Don't you wonder
how people think
the banks of space
and time don't matter?
How they'll drain
the big tanks down to
slime and salamanders
and want thanks?

THAT WILL TO DIVEST

Action creates
a taste
for itself.
Meaning: once
you've swept
the shelves
of spoons
and plates
you kept
for guests,
it gets harder
not to also
simplify the larder,
not to dismiss
rooms, not to
divest yourself
of all the chairs
but one, not
to test what
singleness can bear,
once you've begun.

Winter Fear

Is it just winter
or is this worse.
Is this the year
when outer damp
obscures a deeper curse
that spring can't fix,
when gears that
turn the earth
won't shift the view,
when clouds won't lift
though all the skies
go blue.

GRAZING HORSES

Sometimes the
green pasture
of the mind
tilts abruptly.
The grazing horses
struggle crazily
for purchase
on the frictionless
nearly vertical
surface. Their
furniture-fine
legs buckle
on the incline,
unhorsed by slant
they weren't
designed to climb
and can't.

WASTE

Not even waste
is inviolate.
The day misspent,
the love misplaced,
has inside it
the seed of redemption.
Nothing is exempt
from resurrection.
It is tiresome
how the grass
re-ripens, greening
all along the punched
and mucked horizon
once the bison
have moved on,
leaning into hunger
and hard luck.

FORGETTING

Forgetting takes space.
Forgotten matters displace
as much anything else as
anything else. We must
skirt unlabeled crates
as though it made sense
and take them when we go
to other states.

THE FOURTH WISE MAN

The fourth wise man
disliked travel. If
you walk, there's the
gravel. If you ride,
there's the camel's attitude.
He far preferred
to be inside in solitude
to contemplate the star
that had been getting
so much larger
and more *prolate* lately—
stretching vertically
(like the souls of martyrs)
toward the poles
(or like the yawns of babies).

BEASTS

Time lingers
quietly in attics.
Romantics are
always fingering
some discolored
fabric or other,
feeling a deep
nostalgia for sepia,
a mellow sadness
at what keeps
but yellows.
But other people
don't trust ambering
or court the filigrees
of rust. They've
seen lost greens
of memory ignite,
dead dogs released,
and don't invite
the rainbow beasts.

Gaps

Gaps don't
just happen.
There is a
generative element
inside them,
a welling motion
as when cold
waters shoulder
up through
warmer oceans.
And where gaps
choose to widen,
coordinates warp,
even in places
constant since
the oldest maps.

THE FABRIC OF LIFE

It is very stretchy.
We know that, even if
many details remain
sketchy. It is complexly
woven. That much too
has pretty well been
proven. We are loath
to continue our lessons,
which consist of slaps
as sharp and dispersed
as bee stings from
a smashed nest,
when any strand snaps—
hurts working far past
the locus of rupture,
attacking threads
far beyond anything
we would have said
connects.

HELP

Imagine *help*
as a syllable,
awkward but utterable.

How would it work
and in which distress?
How would one gauge
the level of duress
at which to pitch
the plea? How bad
would something
have to be?

It's hard,
coming from a planet
where if we needed something
we had it.

THE PASS

Even in climes
without snow
one cannot go
forward sometimes.
Things test you.
You are part of
the Donners or
part of the rescue:
a muleteer in
earflaps; a
formerly hearty
midwestern farmer
perhaps. Both
parties trapped
within sight
of the pass.

THE PIECES THAT FALL TO EARTH

One could
almost wish
they wouldn't;
they are so
far apart,
so random.
One cannot
wait, cannot
abandon waiting.
The three or
four occasions
of their landing
never fade.
Should there
be more, there
will never be
enough to make
a pattern
that can equal
the commanding
way they matter.

Don't Look Back

This is not
a problem
for the neckless.
Fish cannot
recklessly
swivel their heads
to check
on their fry;
no one expects
this. They are
torpedoes of
disinterest,
compact capsules
that rely
on the odds
for survival,

unfollowed by
the exact and modest
number of goslings
the S-necked
goose is—
who if she
looks back
acknowledges losses
and if she does not
also loses.

IT'S ALWAYS DARKEST JUST
BEFORE THE DAWN

But how dark
is *darkest*?
Does it get
jet—or tar—
black; does it
glint and increase
in hardness
or turn viscous?
Are there stages
of darkness
and chips
to match against
its increments,
holding them
up to our blindness,
estimating when
we'll have the
night behind us?

Blunt

If we could love
the blunt
and not
the point

we would
almost constantly
have what we want.

What is the
blunt of this
I would ask you

our conversation
weeding up
like the Sargasso.

Diamonds

Is the snail
sharpened
by crawling
over diamonds?
Is her foot
hardened
so it can't
carry her?
No. Snails
make mucus.
Even the
most precious
barriers
to lettuce
are useless.

HERRING

A thousand
tiny silver
thoughtlets
play in the mind,
untarnished
as herring.

They shutter
like blinds,
then sliver,
then utterly
vanish.

Is it unkind
to hope
some will
eat others;
is it uncaring?

THE SILENCE ISLANDS

These are the
Silence Islands,
where what outsiders
would consider
nearly imperceptible
aural amusements
land like coconuts
on the crystalline
hammers and anvils
of the native inhabitants.
Theirs is a refinement
so exquisite that,
for example, to rhyme
anything with *hibiscus*
is interdicted anytime
children or anyone weakened
by sickness is expected.

Cheshire

It's not the cat,
it's the smile that
lasts, toothy
and ruthless.
It's facts like this
we like to resist—
how our parts
may lack allegiance
to the whole;
how the bonds
may be more casual
than we know; how
much of us
might vanish
and how well
some separate part
might manage.

YESES

Just behind
the door,
a second.
But smaller
by a few inches.
Behind which
a third again
diminishes.
Then more
and more,
forming a
foreshortened
corridor or
niche of yeses
ending in
a mouse's
entrance
with a knob
too small
to pinch.

GREAT THOUGHTS

Great thoughts
do not nourish
small thoughts
as parents do children.

Like the eucalyptus,
they make the soil
beneath them barren.

Standing in a
grove of them
is hideous.

TEST

Imagine a surface
so still and vast
that it could test
exactly what
is set in motion
when a single stone
is cast into its ocean.
Possessed of a calm
so far superior
to people's, it alone
could be assessed
ideally irascible.
In such a case,
if ripples yawed
or circles wobbled
in their orbits
like spun plates,
it would be the *law*
and not so personal
that what drops warps
and what warps dissipates.

CROWN

Too much rain
loosens trees.
In the hills giant oaks
fall upon their knees.
You can touch parts
you have no right to—
places only birds
should fly to.

Bad Day

Not every day
is a good day
for the elfin tailor.
Some days
the stolen cloth
reveals what it
was made for:
a handsome weskit
or the jerkin
of an elfin sailor.
Other days
the tailor
sees a jacket
in his mind
and sets about
to find the fabric.
But some days
neither the idea
nor the material
presents itself;
and these are
the hard days
for the tailor elf.

AMONG ENGLISH VERBS

Among English verbs
to die is oddest in its
eagerness to be *dead,*
immodest in its
haste to be told—
a verb alchemical
in the head:
one speck of its gold
and a whole life's lead.

LIME LIGHT

One can't work
by lime light.

A bowlful
right at
one's elbow

produces no
more than
a baleful
glow against
the kitchen table.

The fruit purveyor's
whole unstable
pyramid

doesn't equal
what daylight did.

Why We Must Struggle

If we have not struggled
as hard as we can
at our strongest
how will we sense
the shape of our losses
or know what sustains
us longest or name
what change costs us,
saying how strange
it is that one sector
of the self can step in
for another in trouble,
how loss activates
a latent double, how
we can feed
as upon nectar
upon need?

DROPS IN THE BUCKET

At first
each drop
makes its
own pock
against the tin.
In time
there is a
thin lacquer
which is
layered and
relayered
till there's
a quantity
of water
with its
own skin
and sense
of purpose,
shocked at
each new violation
of its surface.

THE JOB

Imagine that
the job were
so delicate
that you could
seldom—almost
never—remember
it. Impossible
work, really.
Like placing
pebbles exactly
where they were
already. The
steadiness it
takes . . . and
to what end?
It's so easy
to forget again.

Dutch

Much of life
is Dutch
one-digit
operations

in which
legions of
big robust
people crouch

behind
badly cracked
dike systems

attached
by the thumbs

their wide
balloon-pantsed rumps
up-ended to the
northern sun

while, back
in town, little
black-suspendered
tulip magnates
stride around.

CHEMISE

What would the self
disrobed look like,
the form undraped?
There is a flimsy cloth
we can't take off—
some last chemise
we can't escape—
a hope more intimate
than paint
to please.

DEFERRED SILENCE

There is a
deferred silence
which only follows
a deferred sound.
As when an oak falls
when no one is around.
The violence waits
for someone to approach
to have just stopped.
There is that ozone
freshness to the aftershock.

ATTENTION

As strong as
the suction cups
on the octopus
are the valves
of the attention.

If threatened
or pulled off
they leave welts
and pink rings

but also
can unstick
unfelt
from things.

FAILURE

Like slime
inside a
stagnant tank

its green
deepening
from lime
to emerald

a dank
but less
ephemeral
efflorescence

than success
is in general.

MATRIGUPTA

of Ujjain, India, wrote a poem that so pleased Rajah Vicrama Ditya HE WAS GIVEN THE ENTIRE STATE OF KASHMIR. *The poet ruled Kashmir for five years (118–123)* AND THEN ABDICATED TO BECOME A RECLUSE.
—*Ripley's Believe It or Not*

(What a Trojan horse)
thought Matrigupta,
rewarded for his verse
by Rajah Ditya
with one of the nicest
states in India.
(Why couldn't it
have been a gold watch
or an inscribed plate?
I'll never write again
at this rate.)

"I am too blessed,"
went the little thank-you
poem he had rehearsed,
but already his words
were getting reversed
and he said, "I am
blue tressed," which was
only the first indication
of how things were in Kashmir
before his abdication.

Weakness and Doubt

Weakness and doubt
are symbionts
famous throughout
the fungal orders
which admire pallors,
rusts, grey talcums,
the whole palette
of dusts and powders
of the rot kingdom
and do not share
our kind's disgust
at dissolution,
following the
interplay of doubt
and weakness
as a robust
sort of business;
the way we
love construction,
they love hollowing.

Failure 2

There could be nutrients
in failure—
deep amendments
to the shallow soil
of wishes.
Think of the
dark and bitter
flavors of
black ales
and peasant loaves.
Think of licorices.
Think about
the tales of how
Indians put fishes
under corn plants.
Next time hope
relinquishes a form,
think about that.

Two More, and Up Goes the Donkey

An old cry at fairs, the showman having promised his credulous hearers that as soon as enough pennies are collected his donkey will balance himself on the top of a pole or ladder. Always a matter of "two more pennies," the trick is never performed.
—Brewer's Dictionary of Phrase and Fable

Old men
who were boys then
continue to imagine
how it would have been
to see a donkey
balancing above them.
Some see all four
small hooves
compressed on
the post top;
some see one.
It depends upon
which penny
wasn't spent,
which trick
wasn't done.

Water under the Bridge

That's water under
the bridge, we say,
siding with the bridge
and no wonder,
given the sloping ways
of water which
grows so grey
and oily, toiling
slowly downward,
its wide dented
slide ever onward;
we aren't demented.

Your Face Will Stick

However bland we all
begin when picked
from the common
stock of cherubim,
your face will stick.
There will be
a spot at which
you hear the click.
Your baby ears—
pink shells—will
prick, your look grow
pixieish or dour,
fixed upon the
inner notch or
catch you can't resist,
like clocks set up
to strike the hour.

AND ALL BECOMES AS BEFORE

—Martin Buber, *The Legend of the Baal-Shem*

So why do we want to go
if this travel is
so without profit

if not even a souvenir pebble
lodges in a boot waffle

or a half ticket sticks
in the corner of a pocket

if it is so perfect
that it takes every tick
of its private clock back

patting us down at the exit
like a bank dick

pushing us back into traffic?

THE NIAGARA RIVER

2005

THE NIAGARA RIVER

As though
the river were
a floor, we position
our table and chairs
upon it, eat, and
have conversation.
As it moves along,
we notice—as
calmly as though
dining room paintings
were being replaced—
the changing scenes
along the shore. We
do know, we do
know this is the
Niagara River, but
it is hard to remember
what that means.

HOME TO ROOST

The chickens
are circling and
blotting out the
day. The sun is
bright, but the
chickens are in
the way. Yes,
the sky is dark
with chickens,
dense with them.
They turn and
then they turn
again. These
are the chickens
you let loose
one at a time
and small—
various breeds.
Now they have
come home
to roost—all
the same kind
at the same speed.

Carrying a Ladder

We are always
really carrying
a ladder, but it's
invisible. We
only know
something's
the matter:
something precious
crashes; easy doors
prove impassable.
Or, in the body,
there's too much
swing or off-
center gravity.
And, in the mind,
a drunken capacity,
access to out-of-range
apples. As though
one had a way to climb
out of the damage
and apology.

SHARKS' TEETH

Everything contains some
silence. Noise gets
its zest from the
small shark's-tooth-
shaped fragments
of rest angled
in it. An hour
of city holds maybe
a minute of these
remnants of a time
when silence reigned,
compact and dangerous
as a shark. Sometimes
a bit of a tail
or fin can still
be sensed in parks.

WEAK FORCES

I enjoy an accumulating
faith in weak forces—
a weak faith, of course,
easily shaken, but also
easily regained—in what
starts to drift: all the
slow untrainings of the mind,
the sift left of resolve
sustained too long, the
strange internal shift
by which there's no knowing
if this is the road taken
or untaken. There are soft
affinities, possibly electrical;
lint-like congeries; moonlit
hints; asymmetrical pink
glowy spots that are not
the defeat of something,
I don't think.

THE ELEPHANT IN THE ROOM

It isn't so much
a complete elephant
as an elephant
sense—perhaps
pillar legs supporting
a looming mass,
beyond which it's
mostly a guess.
In any case, we
manage with relative
ease. There are just
places in the room
that we bounce off
when we come up
against; not something
we feel we have to
announce.

A Ball Rolls on a Point

The whole ball
of who we are
presses into
the green baize
at a single tiny
spot. An aural
track of crackle
betrays our passage
through the
fibrous jungle.
It's hot and
desperate. Insects
spring out of it.
The pressure is
intense, and the
sense that we've
lost proportion.
As though bringing
too much to bear
too locally were
our decision.

THE BEST OF IT

However carved up
or pared down we get,
we keep on making
the best of it as though
it doesn't matter that
our acre's down to
a square foot. As
though our garden
could be one bean
and we'd rejoice if
it flourishes, as
though one bean
could nourish us.

CHINESE FOOT CHART

Every part of us
alerts another part.
Press a spot in
the tender arch and
feel the scalp
twitch. We are no
match for ourselves
but our own release.
Each touch
uncatches some
remote lock. Look,
boats of mercy
embark from
our heart at the
oddest knock.

SHIPWRECK

*I was shipwrecked beneath a stormless sky
in a sea shallow enough to stand up in.*
—Fernando Pessoa

They're laughable
when we get there—
the ultimate articulations
of despair: trapped
in a tub filling with
our own tears, strapped
to a breadstick mast
a mouse could chew
down, hopping around
the house in paper shackles
wrist and ankle. It's
always stagey. Being
lost is just one's fancy—
some cloth, some paste—
the essence of flimsy.
Therefore we
double don't know
why we don't take off
the Crusoe rags, step
off the island, bow
from the waist, accept
your kudos.

THE OTHER SHOE

Oh if it were
only the other
shoe hanging
in space before
joining its mate.
If the undropped
didn't congregate
with the undropped.
But nothing can
stop the midair
collusion of the
unpaired above us
acquiring density
and weight. We
feel it accumulate.

ATLAS

Extreme exertion
isolates a person
from help,
discovered Atlas.
Once a certain
shoulder-to-burden
ratio collapses,
there is so little
others can do:
they can't
lend a hand
with Brazil
and not stand
on Peru.

HE LIT A FIRE WITH ICICLES

For W. G. Sebald, 1944–2001

This was the work
of St. Sebolt, one
of his miracles:
he lit a fire with
icicles. He struck
them like a steel
to flint, did St.
Sebolt. It
makes sense
only at a certain
body heat. How
cold he had
to get to learn
that ice would
burn. How cold
he had to stay.
When he could
feel his feet
he had to
back away.

Rats' Tails

For Joseph Brodsky, 1940–1996

All that's left of him is rats' tails.
There's a fate I could envy.
—Joseph Brodsky

Let's say
some day
all that's
left of him
is rats' tails,
just scattered
bits of script:
a loose *e*,
an *s* or two,
a *g*, an almost-
n. If he had
hands he'd
rub them as
the test begins:
to see how little
will suggest
the rat again.

Added Significance

In the wake of
horrible events
each act or word
is fortified with
added significance,
unabsorbable as
nutrients added
to the outside
of food: it can't
do any good.
As if significance
weren't burdensome
enough. Now
the wave-slapped
beach rocks not
just made to talk
but made to *teach*.

Chop

The bird
walks down
the beach along
the glazed edge
the last wave
reached. His
each step makes
a perfect stamp—
smallish, but as
sharp as an
emperor's chop.
Stride, stride,
goes the emperor
down his wide
mirrored promenade
the sea bows
to repolish.

FELIX CROW

Crow school
is basic and
short as a rule—
just the rudiments
of *quid pro crow*
for most students.
Then each lives out
his unenlightened
span, adding his
bit of blight
to the collected
history of pushing out
the sweeter species;
briefly swaggering the
swagger of his
aggravating ancestors
down my street.
And every time
I like him
when we meet.

DESERT RESERVOIRS

They are beachless
basins, steep-edged
catches, unnatural
bodies of water wedged
into canyons, stranded
anti-mirages
unable to vanish
or moisten a landscape
of cactus adapted
to thrift, a wasteland
to creatures who chew
one another or grasses
for moisture. Nothing
here matches their gift.

HAILSTORM

Like a storm
of hornets, the
little white planets
layer and relayer
as they whip around
in their high orbits,
getting more and
more dense before
they crash against
our crust. A maelstrom
of ferocious little
fists and punches,
so hard to believe
once it's past.

EXPECTATIONS

We expect rain
to animate this
creek: these rocks
to harbor gurgles,
these pebbles to
creep downstream
a little, those leaves
to circle in the
eddy, the stains
and gloss of wet.
The bed is ready
but no rain yet.

Green Hills

Their green flanks
and swells are not
flesh in any sense
matching ours,
we tell ourselves.
Nor their green
breast nor their
green shoulder nor
the languor of their
rolling over.

Rubbing Lamps

Things besides
Aladdin's and
the golden cave
fish's lamps
grant wishes.
In fact,
most lamps
aren't lamp-
shaped and
happen by
accident: an
ordinary knob
goes lambent
as you twist
or a cloth turns
to silver mesh
against a dish—

something
so odd and
filled with promise
for a minute
that you spend
your only wish
wishing someone else
could see it.

Tenderness and Rot

Tenderness and rot
share a border.
And rot is an
aggressive neighbor
whose iridescence
keeps creeping over.

No lessons
can be drawn
from this however.

One is not
two countries.
One is not meat
corrupting.

It is important
to stay sweet
and loving.

TAR BABIES

Tar babies are
not the children
of tar people.
It is far worse.
The tar baby occurs
spontaneously
nor do we adhere
at first. There is
an especially
unperverse
attractiveness
to the tar baby—
although currently
she is a little sick.
When you start
to help her
is when she
starts to stick.

Tired Blood

Well, not *tired*
so much as *freighted*.
As though foreign objects
had invaded.
As though tiny offices
had dumped
their metal furniture
among the glossy lozenges
and platelets—
chairs that stick together,
painful cabinets.

THEFT

The egg-sucking fox
licks his copper chops.
The shell cups
lie scattered from
the orange debauch.

It is honest
straightforward theft—
unlike whatever
cruel thing
steals *thought*

the full weight left
and the locked room
still locked.

IDEAL AUDIENCE

Not scattered legions,
not a dozen from
a single region
for whom accent
matters, not a seven-
member coven,
not five shirttail
cousins; just
one free citizen—
maybe not alive
now even—who
will know with
exquisite gloom
that only we two
ever found this room.

Caps

People should be
open on top like a cup.
A piece of bread
should be able to sop
some of us up.
We should be milk-like
or like wine. We should
not have to be trying
to get our caps off all the time.
The storybook boy
attempts the simple gesture
of baring his head
for his emperor,
but another hat has appeared.
This happens over and over.
Who does not share
his despair of simplicity,
of acting clearly and with dignity?
And what pleasure can we find
in the caps, brightly feathered
and infinitely various,
that pile up so high they bury us?

Thin

How anything
is known
is so thin—
a skin of ice
over a pond
only birds might
confidently walk
upon. A bird's
worth of weight
or one bird-weight
of Wordsworth.

STARDUST

Stardust is
the hardest thing
to hold out for.
You must
make of yourself
a perfect plane—
something still
upon which
something settles—
something like
sugar grains on
something like
metal, but with
none of the chill.
It's hard to explain.

Blue China Doorknob

I was haunted by the image of a blue china doorknob.
I never used the doorknob, or knew what it meant,
yet somehow it started the current of images.
—Robert Lowell

Rooms may be
using us. We
may be the agents
of doorknobs'
purposes, obeying
imperatives china
dreams up or
pacing dimensions
determined by
cabinets. And if
we're their instruments—
the valves of their
furious trumpets,
conscripted but
ignorant of it—
the strange, unaccountable
things we betray
were never our secrets
anyway.

SALVAGE

The wreck
is a fact.
The worst
has happened.
The salvage trucks
back in and
the salvage men
begin to sort
and stack,
whistling as
they work.
Thanks be
to God—again—
for extractable elements
which are not
carriers of pain,
for this periodic
table at which
the self-taught
salvagers disassemble
the unthinkable
to the unthought.

THE LIGHT OF INTERIORS

The light of interiors
is the admixture
of who knows how many
doors ajar, windows
casually curtained,
unblinded or opened,
oculi set into ceilings,
wells, ports, shafts,
loose fits, leaks,
and other breaches
of surface. But, in
any case, the light,
once in, bounces
toward the interior,
glancing off glassy
enamels and polishes,
softened by the scuffed
and often-handled, muffled
in carpet and toweling,
buffeted down hallways,

baffled equally
by scatter and order
to an ideal and now
sourceless texture which,
when mixed with silence,
makes of a simple
table with flowers
an island.

THINGS SHOULDN'T BE SO HARD

A life should leave
deep tracks:
ruts where she
went out and back
to get the mail
or move the hose
around the yard;
where she used to
stand before the sink,
a worn-out place;
beneath her hand
the china knobs
rubbed down to
white pastilles;
the switch she
used to feel for
in the dark
almost erased.
Her things should
keep her marks.
The passage
of a life should show;

it should abrade.
And when life stops,
a certain space—
however small—
should be left scarred
by the grand and
damaging parade.
Things shouldn't
be so hard.

THE PAST

Sometimes there's
suddenly no way
to get from
one part to
another, as though
the past were
a frozen lake
breaking up. But
not from the
top; not because
it's warmer
up here; it's not.
But from underneath
for some reason—
perhaps some heat
trapped on its own
for so long it's
developed seasons.

REVERSE DRAMA

Lightning, but not bright.
Thunder, but not loud.
Sometimes something
in the sky connects
to something in the ground
in ways we don't expect
and more or less miss except
through reverse drama:
things were heightened
and now they're calmer.

Fake Spots

Like air
in rocks, fake
spots got here
really far back.
Everything is
part caulk.
Some apartments
in apartment blocks
are blanks;
some steeples
are shims. Also
in people: parts
are wedges: and,
to the parts they keep
apart, *precious.*

LEGERDEMAIN

Some days one gets
the *in* but not
the *out* part of the
rabbit/hat trick.
And the longer
a creature stays,
the worse it sticks.
Dispatch means
so much, one
remembers again.
A thing can get
too conjured
for legerdemain.

Hide and Seek

It's hard not
to jump out
instead of
waiting to be
found. It's
hard to be
alone so long
and then hear
someone come
around. It's
like some form
of skin's developed
in the air
that, rather
than have torn,
you tear.

Post-Construction

Who knows better
than the builder
not to trust
a structure, where
it's off kilter,
how too few
rafters bear
too much roof?

And still it
may stand, proof
against craft,
strong as though
ghost ribs
had been added
after one left.

LEAST ACTION

Is it vision
or the lack
that brings me
back to the principle
of least action,
by which in one
branch of rabbinical
thought the world
might become the
Kingdom of Peace not
through the tumult
and destruction necessary
for a New Start but
by adjusting little parts
a little bit—turning
a cup a quarter inch
or scooting up a bench.
It imagines an
incremental resurrection,
a radiant body
puzzled out through

tinkering with the fit
of what's available.
As though what is is
right already but
askew. It is tempting
for any person who would
like to love what she
can do.

CHART

There is a big
figure, your age,
crawling, then
standing, now
beginning to bend
as he crosses
the stage. Or
she. A blurred
and generalized
projection of you
and me. For a
long time it seems
as remote
from the self
as the ape chart
where they rise up
and walk into man.
And then it seems
the realer part.

No Names

There are high places
that don't invite us,
sharp shapes, glacier-
scraped faces, whole
ranges whose given names
slip off. Any such relation
as we try to make
refuses to take. Some
high lakes are not for us,
some slick escarpments.
I'm giddy with thinking
where thinking can't stick.

THE MATERIAL

*The ratio between the material Cornell collected
and the material that ended up in his boxes
was probably a thousand to one.*
—Deborah Solomon, *Utopia Parkway*

Whatever is done
leaves a hole in the
possible, a snip in
the gauze, a marble
and thimble missing
from the immaterial.
The laws are cruel
on this point. The
undone can't be
patched or stretched.
The wounds last.
The bundles of
nothing that are
our gift at birth, the
lavish trains we
trail into our span
like vans of seamless
promise, like fresh
sheets in baskets,

are our stock. We
must extract parts
to do work. As
time passes, the
promise tatters
like a battle flag
above a war we
hope mattered.

THE WELL OR THE CUP

How can
you tell
at the start
what you
can give away
and what
you must hold
to your heart.
What is
the well
and what is
a cup. Some
people get
drunk up.

LATE JUSTICE

Late justice may
be more useless
than none. Some
expungings or
making-rights
or getting-backs
lack the capacity
to correct. The
formerly aggrieved
become exacting
in unattractive
ways: intolerant
of delay, determined
to collect. And shocked—
shocked—at their
new unappeasableness,
who had so long
been so reasonable.

BACKWARD MIRACLE

Every once in a while
we need a
backward miracle
that will strip language,
make it *hold* for
a minute: just the
vessel with the
wine in it—
a sacramental
refusal to multiply,
reclaiming the
single loaf
and the single
fish thereby.

Green Behind the Ears

I was still slightly
fuzzy in shady spots
and the tenderest lime.
It was lovely, as I
look back, but not
at the time. For it is
hard to be green and
take your turn as flesh.
So much freshness
to unlearn.

THIEVES

There are thieves
in the mind, their
dens in places
we'd prefer
not to know.
When a word
is lifted from
its spot, we show
no surprise,
replacing *supplies*
with *provender*.
Out here, it's
the tiniest stutter,
the subtlest patch—
an affordable loss
of no significance
whatever to the
plastic surface of
social commerce.
Should a bit vanish
from an event, we

likewise manage.
But back at the ranch,
a hoard is building.
The thieves are
hatching some
fantastic plot
made out of parts
we'd laugh to think
that they thought
matched.

LIGHTHOUSE KEEPING

Seas pleat
winds keen
fogs deepen
ships lean no
doubt, and
the lighthouse
keeper keeps
a light for
those left out.
It is intimate
and remote both
for the keeper
and those afloat.

TUNE

Imagine a sea
of ultramarine
suspending a
million jellyfish
as soft as moons.
Imagine the
interlocking uninsistent
tunes of drifting things.
This is the deep machine
that powers the lamps
of dreams and accounts
for their bluish tint.
How can something
so grand and serene
vanish again and again
without a hint?

Index

tinkering with the fit
of what's available.
As though what is is
right already but
askew. It is tempting
for any person who would
like to love what she
can do.

CHART

There is a big
figure, your age,
crawling, then
standing, now
beginning to bend
as he crosses
the stage. Or
she. A blurred
and generalized
projection of you
and me. For a
long time it seems
as remote
from the self
as the ape chart
where they rise up
and walk into man.
And then it seems
the realer part.